IMAGES
of England

AROUND
TAMWORTH

A group posing in front of their float waiting to take part in the Tamworth Hospital Carnival, some time during the 1940s. It is just possible to make out on the tins they are holding the words Tamworth Hospital Carnival. The first town carnival took place in 1931 and raised around £600 for the hospital.

IMAGES
of England

AROUND
TAMWORTH

Compiled by
Chris Gibson

TEMPUS

First published 2000
Copyright © Chris Gibson, 2000

Tempus Publishing Limited
The Mill, Brimscombe Port,
Stroud, Gloucestershire, GL5 2QG

ISBN 0 7524 1873 4

Typesetting and origination by
Tempus Publishing Limited
Printed in Great Britain by
Midway Clark Printing, Wiltshire

The flag flys on the castle in 1913 as the crowds gather around the bandstand in the castle grounds. Note that the steep banks either side of the bandstand have not yet been laid out as flowerbeds as they are today. The occasion is unknown but there is at least one other photographer, with his tripod and large bag, on hand to record proceedings. He can be seen on the bottom left of the picture.

Contents

Introduction   7

1.   Local Schools   9
2.   Places of Worship   19
3.   St Editha's Parish Church   27
4.   Entertainment   33
5.   A Sporting Life   45
6.   Market Street   51
7.   Drayton Manor and other Desirable Residences   59
8.   The Castle and Grounds   77
9.   Around the Town   87
10.   Hopwas and Hints   101
11.   Other Local Village Scenes   107

Miss Ivy Allsopp can be seen here during the crowning ceremony for the Tamworth Carnival Queen. She was the 1932 carnival queen and was only the second young lady to be honoured with the title. The Mayor of Tamworth, Mr G.H. Jones, bestowed the crown in front of a large crowd of around 2,000 people on that warm July evening in the castle grounds. Amington Band provided additional musical entertainment.

Introduction

The photographs in this book have all been taken from my collection of local postcards depicting Tamworth and the surrounding villages. I have been building this collection for a number of years and it is still steadily growing.

Many of the pictures for the cards were taken by local photographers, most notably the father and son from the Weale family whose studio portrait business thrived in Victoria Road, Tamworth. As well as supplying images for use on postcards, many Weale images also appear in various contemporary books published about the area.

Local businesses would often have adveritsments for their services printed onto the backs of cards produced by national publishers such as Valentine and Frith. Most of the cards in this book date from around the turn of the century, the so-called Golden Age of the Picture Postcard. During this period literally millions of cards were sent each year and a great many people indulged in the hobby of postcard collecting, the messages on the reverse of many cards bear this fact out.

Two of the most important buildings in the town, the castle and St Editha's church, not surprisingly featured on a large number of cards through the years, as were many of the town centre streets, most notably George Street and Market Street. I have tried where possible to include images that have not been previously published in similar books of this nature.

Although all pictures printed in this book are in black and white, many of the original cards were produced in colour, and often the same view is to be found printed in both colour and black and white versions.

Along with the pictures of Tamworth there are also many views of the villages within a five mile radius of the town. Tamworth would have been the focal point for many of these smaller villages, due to its wider range of shops and facilities not available in the villages. At the turn of the century when transport, both public and private, was not as accessible as it is today people would have often had to walk into the town from these out-lying places.

The town's history is a long and colourful one. During medieval times the town was the capital of Mercia under the Kingship of King Offa. It was Offa who fortified the town against invasion by constructing a large ditch around it. Ethelfleda, known as the Lady of the Mercians, also put later fortifications in place in 913. There are several pictures included here of the 1000th anniversary celebrations of Ethelfleda's efforts on behalf of Tamworth.

Other notable residents of the area include Sir Robert Peel, the prime minister who delivered the famous Tamworth Manifesto from the Town Hall in Market Street. The Town Hall was built by another well-known Tamworthian, Thomas Guy, the man who founded Guy's Hospital in London.

I have tried to ensure that all the information contained in the captions in this book is as accurate as possible. I would be interested to hear from readers who have other information relating to these pictures or who may have old photographs of Tamworth themselves. Please contact me, I would be glad to hear from you.

Chris Gibson
PO Box 3292
Tamworth
Staffs
B77 4BA
Email kiffg@bigfoot.com

Church Street, shown here around 1910. One of Tamworth's oldest pubs, The Stone Cross, is in the foreground on the right.

One
Local Schools

Thomas Barnes originally founded this school at Hopwas in 1724. The building in the picture was built and named after him in 1909. The picture was taken around 1932.

Tamworth Grammar School is believed to be amongst the ten oldest schools in the country. The school was granted a charter by Queen Elizabeth in 1588 and became known as The Free Grammar School of Elizabeth, Queen of England. The school dates back much further than this though and is thought to have formed part of the college supposedly founded in Tamworth in 963 by King Edgar. The buildings shown here are part of the present day school c. 1912.

The buildings shown here in 1912 still form part of the present day grammar school complex. This site was first established in 1867 when the school moved from its former site in Lower Gungate. Sir John Bowes of Elford gave the site in Lower Gungate in 1594. The buildings of 1867 were further added to in 1904 and 1910.

Classes one and two of St. Benedict's School, Dordon pose here for their school photograph, c. 1926.

Lichfield Street in 1908. The building on the left of the picture was one of the schools funded by Sir Robert Peel. This school was built when the previous building on the opposite side of the road (not in the picture) became too small. Both buildings are still in existence.

NETHERSOLE SCHOOL, POLESWORTH.

A splendid building that forms part of Nethersole School, shown here in 1901. The school was named after its founder Sir Francis Nethersole who set up the school in 1638.

The original Nethersole School was rebuilt during the early 1800s and catered for both boys and girls. It is possible that the photographer has recorded one of the young pupils here in the foreground of this picture as he strides away at the end of another day, c. 1907.

The entrance to St Joseph's Convent school during the 1920s, with its fine stone pillars flanking the doorway. This was the sight that greeted many a nervous pupil on her first visit to the school.

Horse riding was part of the curriculum for the girls lucky enough to be attending this school in the 1930s.

13

The tennis courts shown in this picture from the 1930s certainly seem to have been popular with the girls from St Joseph's.

This new wing to the school, photographed in the 1930s, was opened in July 1932.

The recreation room, pictured during the 1930s, was no doubt a welcome refuge for the girls after a hard day's lessons.

The lounge in the convent at Haunton Hall, again shown in the 1930s, must have been a very pleasant place to while away an hour or two at the end of the day

St Joseph's Convent, Haunton pictured from the air during the 1940s or 50s. This shows the full extent of the buildings of this really quite large complex. At the time this picture was taken it appears there may have been further building work being undertaken as in the top right of the picture it is possible to see a large number of drainage pipes piled up in a field.

7 — Girl's High School, Tamworth

Tamworth Girls High School had its opening ceremony on 1 October 1913. The Countess Ferrers carried out this duty. Also in attendance were William Macgregor, one of the town's great benefactors, and Ald. J.K. Bourne. The groundsman can be seen here in the on this postcard dutifully rolling the grass on the school games field during the 1930s. The grounds of the school covered around four acres in all and comprised of both hard and grass tennis courts and the playing field.

The hall and gymnasium at Tamworth Girls High School in the 1930s. The gym was fitted out with the finest equipment, manufactured in Sweden.

Tamworth Girls High School, shown here between 1930 and 1940, was extended in 1929 to provide more facilities. The hall was enlarged and more room was provided for the younger intake of the school.

The couple charged with the care of the school around this time were Mr and Mrs Day. They were the caretakers from 1923 until 1959

Part of the prefabricated buildings that form Wilnecote High School. The building in the foreground was used as the lower school hall and dining room when the author attended here in the early 1970s. This view was taken from the school playing field.

Two
Places of Worship

Wesleyan Methodist Temple Tamworth

This splendid building, pictured in 1906, was opened with great ceremony in 1877. The celebrations included a choir singing from the rooftop. Prior to the opening of this building, at a cost of £3,500, the Methodist congregation worshipped in a chapel in Bolebridge Street. All of the houses to the left of the temple are still in existence but the one on the right is no longer there.

The church that never was. An illustration from 1909 of a proposed design for a new church in Tamworth that was never built to this particular design.

HOLY TRINITY CHURCH, WILNECOTE.

Wilnecote Holy Trinity church was rebuilt in 1821. It was constructed from brick faced with stone and the church registers date from 1837. Wilnecote became a parish in 1856. In 1882 new seating was installed in the church and it was possible to seat 350 people there. It is shown here in the 1930s.

St Chads Church, pictured during the 1930s, was built in 1879/81. It was designed by John Douglas, an architect from Chester.

St Chad's was consecrated on April 23rd 1881 by Bishop MacLagan who later in his career went on to become the Archbishop of York. This picture is from the 1930s

St Leonard's church, Dordon in 1930. Miss Chetwynd laid the foundation stone for this church on 6 November 1867. She was the daughter of Sir George Chetwynd who had donated the land for the buiding.

The interior of the church, depicted here in 1915 has benefited over the years from the generosity of the congregation. In 1897 the lectern was given as a memorial to Miss Chetwynd and in 1902 the pulpit was given by children from the Sunday school that was held in the church.

St Matthews church, Harlaston with its timber-framed belfry. There has been a church on this site for hundreds of years and the church registers date back to 1693. As was usual on these occasions a large number of village children turned out to get themselves into the photograph, c. 1907.

Harlaston church and post office pictured in 1929. The post office on the right of this picture appears to have a hand-painted sign above the door declaring its presence to any strangers passing through, such as the writer of this postcard who states on the back to his daughters, 'I have been working at this place today'. Trade directories for the area from the 1880s show that the post office/shop was kept by Thomas Sutton, while John Sudbury ran the local pub, the White Lion.

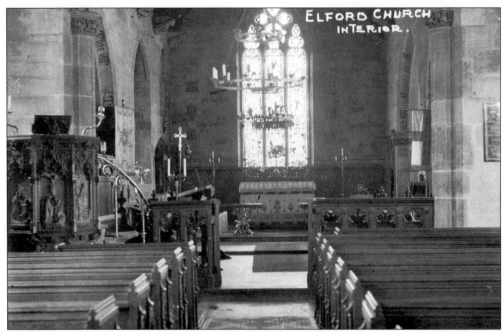

The Elford church clock was paid for by its parishioners in the early 1800s. A further generous gift was received in 1849 when Mr T.Levett, who lived at Elford House, gave the church a new set of six bells. This interior picture was taken around 1925.

The tower of Elford church dates from 1598 while the remainder was rebuilt during the mid 1800s by various architects. One of the more unusual effigies in the church is that of a young boy named John Stanley. He was apparently killed by a blow to the head from a tennis ball in around 1460. The game of tennis played then was quite different from the modern game we know today and the tennis balls probably much harder. This picture was taken in 1920.

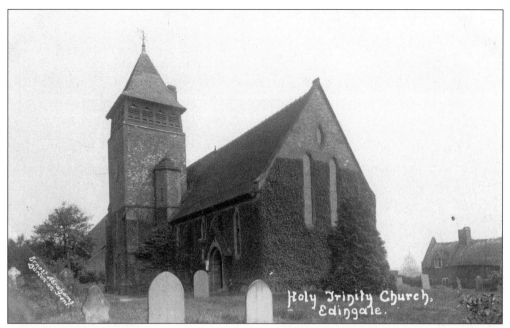

Edingale church, shown here in 1915, was built in 1880 and formally opened on 24 February 1881. The two bells and the clock in the tower were donated in 1884 by relatives of the vicar W.G Garland.

St Andrew's church in Clifton Campville, photographed in the 1920s, dates from the fourteenth century and is one of the finest churches in Staffordshire.

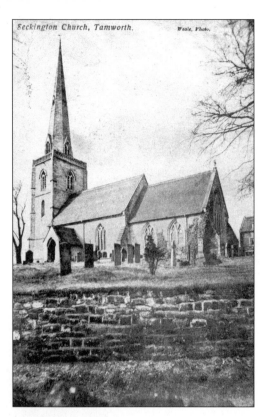

Seckington church dates from the twelfth century. However Seckington is probably best known for an event that happened there some centuries earlier. In AD 757 Ethelbald, the King of the Mercians for over forty years, was killed by one of his own men and his cousin, Offa, best known of the Mercian kings, came to power. This photograph dates from 1908.

The vicarage at Newton Regis seen here with a huge conservatory built onto the rear. The vicar and a small child are standing among what appear to be croquet hoops, *c.* 1910.

Three
St Editha's Parish Church

An early view of St Editha's from the churchyard in 1902. The young saplings shown in this picture are now fine mature specimens in the garden of rest that this former graveyard has become.

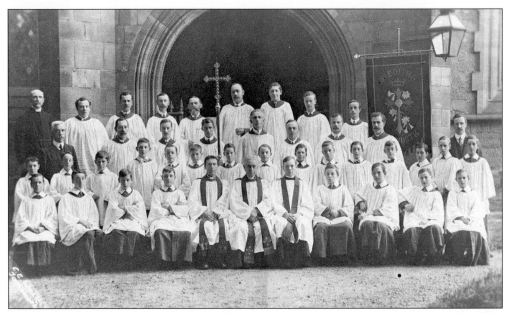

The choir from St Editha's church. William MacGregor can be seen on the far left of the picture in the back row. Seated in the centre of the front row is the Revd J.H. Courtney Clarke. He was vicar from 1896 to 1915. This photograph was taken by the prolific local photographer C.E Weale in the early 1900s.

Members of the clergy pose solemnly for their photograph outside St Editha's parish church. The gentleman seated front row centre is the Revd J.H Courtney Clarke. This picture dates from between 1903 and 1915.

A postcard depicting the churchyard in 1900 before all of the gravestones were taken up and moved. The porch on the side of the church shown here looks very different today now that earlier 'restoration' work has been rectified.

The high church wall, railings and iron gates have now gone from this scene, pictured in 1905. Gone too are the windows that can be seen flung open on the left of the picture. These belonged to the ancient Paregoric Shop that stood in Church Street for hundreds of years. The building on the right of the picture is the Vergery that was purchased by the church in 1882.

Looking towards the chancel in St Editha's. The wrought iron screen seen here in 1908 is thought to have originated in Italy. The large brass-eagle lectern just visible in the centre of the picture dates from 1875 and was a gift to the church.

The timeless interior of St Editha's parish church, seen here in all its glory in 1908. The font in the centre of the picture was a gift to the church from the children of the parish in 1853. It was designed by Sir Gilbert Scott.

The unusual arrangement of the spiral staircase in St Editha's church means that two people can climb both up and down the tower at the same time but never cross each others path. This staircase is usually open once a year to the public who can make the climb to the roof for a small fee. The views from the top are well worth the effort. This postcard dates from 1912.

The Chancel, Tamworth Church.

This photographic postcard helps to show off some of the finer details in the chancel of St Editha's church. The arches on the left date from the fourteenth century. The writer of this postcard in 1914 tells his or her friend how good the choir is in this church and how well behaved they all are.

S. EDITHA'S
Home & Foreign Missions.

SALE OF WORK
FROM 6 TO 10 P.M., ON
WEDNESDAY, NOVEMBER 8TH,
in the
ASSEMBLY ROOMS.

Opening Concert . . .
. . commence 7 p.m.

Evening Pass 6d.

Here is an example of an advertisment printed onto the back of a postcard. This fundraising event would have been based around home baked cakes and other examples of home-made crafts for sale.

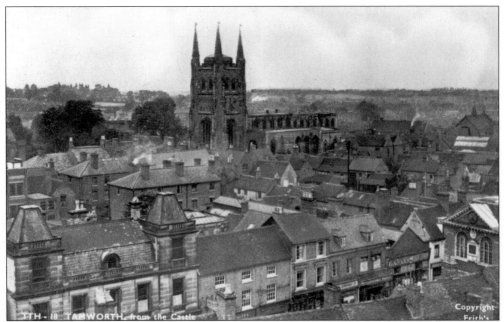

St Editha's pictured here from the castle in the 1940s with Market Street in the foreground. This gives a good idea of the scale of the church and shows how it dominates the rest of the buildings around it.

Four
Entertainment

E CAMP. WHITTINGTON BARRACKS LICHFIELD. (PHOTO. W. MILLS 1914)

Massed troops on the camp ground at Whittington Barracks near Tamworth in 1914. The band can clearly be seen preparing for some sort of concert. Some of their instruments and music sheets are strewn on the ground on the right of the picture. On the rear of this card someone has neatly written the following - West Yorks Militia in Camp on Whittington Heath June 1914.

A very busy Holloway can be seen here with crowds of people thronging the street. The presence of the small wooden ticket booth on the right near the lodge entrance would suggest that some kind of public entertainment was taking place in the castle grounds, which were to be illuminated in the evening, c. 1907.

Some of the 'Grand Illuminations' mentioned on a card from the same series can be seen here. The sender of this card states on the back, 'This is where I was on Saturday. Just 34 miles took us two and a half hours'. The card dates from 1907.

Details of all the entertainment offered by Joshua Dyson's Gypsy Choir when they visited Tamworth's Assembly Rooms in the early 1900s

Joshua Dyson's Gipsy Choir pose for the camera in all their finery. Travelling companies like this would often visit the Assembly Rooms in Tamworth during the early 1900s, putting on various colourfully described shows.

35

This is a publicity card produced to promote Miss Maggie Morton and Company's production of *Home Sweet Home*, c. 1907.

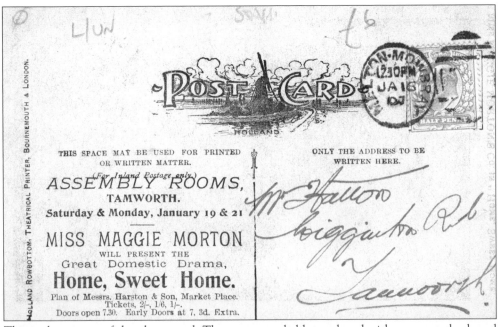

POST CARD

HOLLAND

HOLLAND ROWBOTTOM, THEATRICAL PRINTER, BOURNEMOUTH & LONDON.

THIS SPACE MAY BE USED FOR PRINTED OR WRITTEN MATTER.

(For Inland Postage only.)

ASSEMBLY ROOMS,
TAMWORTH.

Saturday & Monday, January 19 & 21

MISS MAGGIE MORTON
WILL PRESENT THE
Great Domestic Drama,

Home, Sweet Home.

Plan of Messrs. Harston & Son, Market Place.
Tickets, 2/-, 1/6, 1/-.
Doors open 7.30. Early Doors at 7, 3d. Extra.

ONLY THE ADDRESS TO BE WRITTEN HERE.

This is the reverse of the above card. These were probably produced with an empty back and then over-printed by a local printing company with the relevant details for that town's performances.

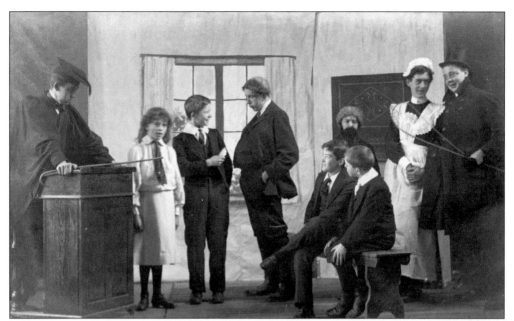

A scene from *Vice Versa*, also known as *A lesson to Fathers*, by F Anstey (1856-1934). This was the grammar school Christmas play in 1910.

A somewhat sleepy scene from the grammar school play of 1911.

A further scene from the same unknown play at the grammar school in 1911.

A play or rehearsal in progress at the Assembly Rooms in Tamworth. By the look of the participants this was possibly a school or a youth group production. They appear to have been rehearsing a musical show as there is a pianist accompanying the cast. The photographer has dated the picture on the back as 16 March 1922.

A snapshot that was probably taken at the Pit Revels that was held at Hall End Hall in July 1910. The Pit Revels were possibly some kind of fun day organised by one of the local colliery ownerse who lived at Hall End Hall.

The group of dancers shown here was the inspiration of Mrs May Trotter, the Revd John Trotter's wife. She did much to revive old customs with plays and dancing. This card was posted just six weeks after the event took place in 1911.

Local dignitaries gather for the unveiling ceremony of the new statue of Ethelfleda in the castle grounds on Wednesday 9 July 1913. The honours were performed by the 11th Earl Ferrers.

'Ethelfleda & Athelstan'
Millenary Memorial, Tamworth Castle.

A close-up look the statue of Ethelfleda and Athelstan in 1913, before it was mounted on its plinth and assumed its present position in the castle grounds. The statue was designed by local stonemason Henry Charles Mitchell and carved by another local man, Edward George Bramwell. Besides being an accomplished stonemason Mitchell was also an expert on the local history of Tamworth. He wrote several books on the subject and also contributed a column to the *Tamworth Herald* on local history. Many of his articles can still be found in the town's local history collection in a series of scrapbooks.

Ox Roasting. Tamworth Millenary.

A bell to draw attention to this ox roasting was probably not really required as the aroma must have spread far and wide to draw in the crowds. The roasting took place on Saturday 12 July 1913, the last day of the Tamworth Millenary celebrations. The beef was ready to eat at 12 noon.

Ox Roasting. Tamworth Millenary.

Over £400 was raised by public subscription to help stage the Millenary celebrations in the town. These celebrations included a parade and a public luncheon with the mayor of the town in the Assembly Rooms. As well as these events there was a Morris dancing exhibition and a band playing in the castle grounds. There were also illuminations in the castle grounds. One day, Thursday 10 July was set aside as Children's Day and all activities on this day were aimed at the youngsters of the town. The preparations to roast the great ox began early on July 12 with the fire being lit at 5.30am in order to ensure the meat was ready for noon.

Basting the Ox. Tamworth Millenary

The roasting of the ox took place opposite the Assembly Rooms on a grassed area, which now forms part of the modern day taxi rank and car park. Members of the public could take a turn at basting the ox for a charge of 1d.

This is the sight that greeted excited villagers at Polesworth on the day that Mr Claude Grahame-White's plane landed there in April 1910. He was forced down by strong winds during his second attempt at winning the London to Manchester Air Race. The prize money was £10,000 a very substantial sum indeed at the turn of the century. Despite two gallant attempts, the prize eluded him and he was beaten by a Frenchman, Louis Paulhan

Claude Graham-White pictured here in 1910, during the first of his two attempts for the prize on offer from the *Daily Mail*. On both occasions he landed at Hademore, which is about three miles north west of Tamworth. On this attempt soldiers from Whittington Barracks were supposed to tie the plane down for the night. However this was not done and the plane was blown over by strong winds and damaged, so ending his first endeavor.

Two men seen here indulging in the popular pastime of punting on the river Tame at Elford, *c.* 1907.

Crowded castle grounds with all the ladies in their best hats and the gents in their straw boaters waiting for an afternoon of entertainment from the band in the bandstand, c. 1912.

This is the boathouse that used to be located in the castle grounds. Lady Bridge is just a little further over to the right of this scene from the 1930s. This spot in the castle grounds near the junction of Tamworth's two rivers is now a favourite place for people to feed the Tamworth swan herd.

Five
A Sporting Life

Bolehall & Glascote W.M.C.
Local Record

A fine display of trophies here for Bolehall and Glascote Working Men's Club. The large case at the back contains what would appear to be the Tamworth and District Air Force Challenge Shield although the writing on the case is somewhat difficult to see. The small cup at the front of the picture has a date of 1906 engraved on it. The picture was taken some time between 1920 and 1945.

Kingsbury Church Lads Brigade cricket team is pictured here in 1907. They were the visiting team although the venue is unknown.

The tug of war team here putting their backs into it at the Tamworth Grammar School sports day in 1911.

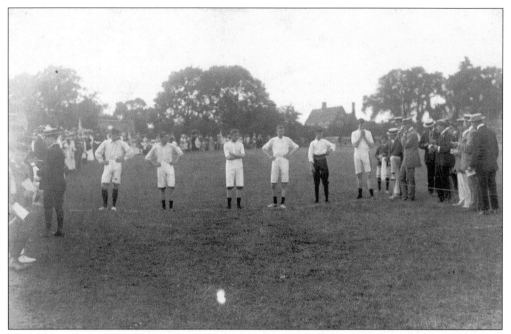

Here the competitors are lined up ready for the start of the half mile race at Tamworth Grammar School sports day in 1911. Taking part were, Wallace, Brain, Westbury, Richardson, Mitchell and Horrocks.

The Half Mile race is underway here and the field is well spread out! Horrocks was first in a time of three minutes forty five seconds while Westbury was second and Richardson was third.

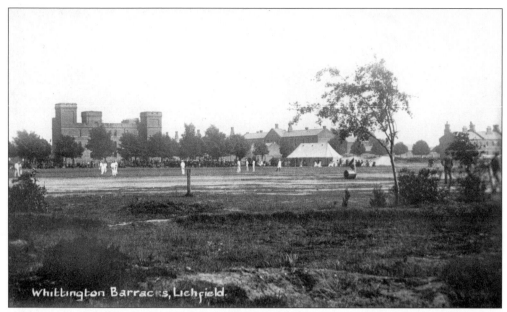

Soldiers relaxing with a cricket match at Whittington Barracks, *c.* 1910.

The hunting party shown here gathered outside Canwell Hall. At the time of this photograph, 1912, hunting was not the controversial subject it is today.

A football team from Polesworth pictured here when they went to play a match against Bewdley in 1914.

The lads from the Tamworth 1st XV 1934/35 are pictured here in the castle grounds. Judging by the state of the muddy kit some of them are wearing, this was an after match photocall, c. 1934.

TAMWORTH . CASTLE . CHURCH & GARDENS.

A tennis match in full swing with the umpire seated precariously on his high seat in the middle of the picture. Throughout the 1930s Tamworth held an annual tennis tournament.

Six
Market Street

TOWN HALL, TAMWORTH.   G. 183.

On the right-hand side of this shot at No. 30 Market Street is the Art and Needlework Repositroy of Mrs Sally Bartle. She previously had a shop at No. 56 Church Street. From both of these locations she sold a series of postcards of the town that she published. At the far end of the street on the left of the Town Hall can be seen the billiard hall run by the Rose Brothers at No. 20 Market Street. The photograph is from around 1938.

On the left of this picture from 1902 is a drapers and hosiery shop although the name is not clear. The building behind and to the right of the town hall has a sign above the door stating Refreshment Rooms.

The town hall and Peel monument. Note the early motorcar on the right of the picture, *c.* 1900.

Market Street with the market in progress during 1912. On the right at No. 5 Market Street is Frederick George Allton's grocers and provisions store. The girl on the right with a basket on her arm is standing outside Alfred Dyer's confectionery and bakers shop that was at No. 34 Market Street. On the left the sign for the Market Vaults pub can be seen.

Thomas Allkins chemist's shop is decorated here for some special occasion, probably the Coronation of King George V in 1911. This shop was here for many years and is still recognisable today because the shop front with its distinctive arches and columns has remained relatively unchanged.

The butter market was held underneath the town hall in days gone by. This picture shows the rather poor state of the stonework in 1912. This has however recently been restored to its former glory. Through the arches on the right of this picture part of the sign for George Fitelson's Bazaar can be seen.

An early Tilling Stevens petrol electric omnibus, pictured in Market Street during the 1920s. The first buses in Tamworth appeared in 1913. The sign on the front of this vehicle shows it is from Coalville and Measham.

A bustling scene in Market Street, taken appropriately on a market day in 1930. The Market Vaults pub can be clearly seen on the left of the picture with Morton's shoe shop on the opposite side of the street. The shop with the blinds pulled down on the left of the picture was Coleman's the ironmongers. Felton Bros. the town's other ironmongers can be seen on the right, next door but one to Morton's.

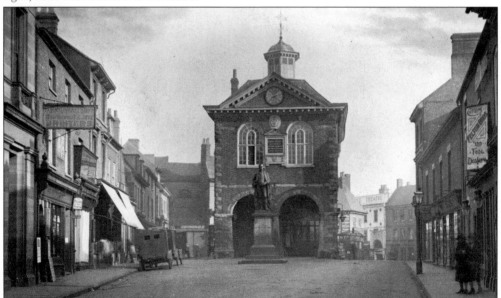

Three old vans are visible here outside these thriving Market Street businesses in 1926. Identifiable establishments include, on the left, Johnson and Allsopp the printers and Land's the chemists. At the end of the street is Jennings the wholesale grocers and druggists. On the right-hand side are Felton Brothers cutlers and tool dealers at No. 28 and 29. At No. 27 was Francis Henry Bramall hatter and hosier. On the same side further into the distance can be seen the Palace Cinema in George Street. An amusing message on the back of this card reads as follows, 'The photo did not come out at all with no sun being out all we can see is the dustbin in the corner of your yard'.

The arches under the town hall have served many purposes over the years. As a market, a store for the town's old fire engine and also as an air raid shelter when the gaps under the arches were filled with sandbags. This picture is from 1908.

A postcard from 1903 showing the town hall and Market Street. The town hall was built in 1701 by Thomas Guy who was a great benefactor to the town. Along with the town hall he also built the almshouses in Lower Gungate, although the buildings there today are the modern replacements for Guy's originals. The shop in the background on the left of the town hall belonged to John Jennings, a long established grocer.

Town Hall, Market St. Tamworth.

A fine selection of old vehicles are on display here in Market Street, some time between 1940 and 1950. Next to the Market Vaults pub is the imposing facade of the National and Provincial Bank. Close inspection of the van on the left of the photograph reveals the name S Jones. A sign for the Beehive Stores can clearly be seen on the right of the picture.

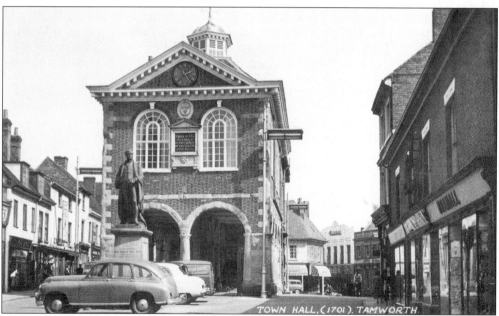

TOWN HALL, (1701). TAMWORTH.

A later view of Market Street, probably from the early 1950s. On the right-hand side the houses and shops that were in George Street have now been replaced with newer buildings for Lloyds Bank and Burtons clothes shop. Many of the old shops on the left have also been replaced by modern ones.

Market Street from the castle. To the left of the Town Hall can be seen the long narrow roof of Fitelson's Bazaar which ran all the way through from Market Street into Church Street. In the background of the picture, behind the church, areas of greenery that have now been built on are clearly visible, c. 1912.

Seven

Drayton Manor and other Desirable Residences

Drayton Manor photographed here from one of its sweeping lawns showing the huge glass houses (right), c. 1906.

The Clock Tower at Drayton Manor in 1905, this is now all that remains of the once magnificent house. The anchor in the picture is now in the castle grounds in Tamworth. Capt. William Peel, who was the third son of Sir Robert Peel, the prime minister, brought this souvenir back from the Crimean War.

The conservatory seen here was added onto the house by the 3rd Sir Robert Peel. This must have been a wonderful place to relax in with the sounds of the trickling fountain and the calls of exotic birds that occupied the place. The photograph dates from 1910.

The renowned architect Robert Smirke, who also designed the British Museum in London, built Drayton Manor.

The sumptuous drawing room at Drayton Manor, pictured in 1905, gives an idea of the splendour in which Sir Robert Peel, the prime minister, lived during his time at the house.

Part of the magnificent gardens at Drayton Manor, seen here in 1904. In their heyday the gardens and grounds were home to all kinds of exotic animals, plants and birds.

The magnificent Statesman's Gallery with its grand marble columns and extensive collection of paintings, *c.* 1910.

The 4th Baronet Peel, grandson of the prime minister, built this splendid Swiss lodge. He built it for his Swiss wife Mercedes de Graffenreid who he married in 1898.

Bonehill House, another fine house with connections to the Peel family, pictured in 1909. The house was built by Edmund Peel, younger brother of Sir Robert Peel. Edmund ran a stud farm at Bonehill.

The extremely well-stocked library in Drayton Manor.

Another aspect of the great house is shown here in 1904. On the far right of the picture is the Clock Tower. The tower is the only surviving relic of this once great house as the main house was pulled down in the 1920s and much of it sold for salvage.

Drayton Manor viewed from across the lake that once formed part of the majestic grounds to the house, *c.* 1906. Closer examination reveals people taking in the view from a lakeside bench on the left of the picture.

A slightly earlier view than the one above in which the lake appears to be much narroweer.

A flurry of activity here at Hints Hall in 1905, as a multitude of carriages, horses and even a bicycle throng the driveway. On the top left of the picture a girl can just be seen sitting precariously on a window ledge, taking in the scene.

The sweeping driveway leading to Hints Hall, which once boasted beautiful water gardens in its grounds. This magnificent house was once home to the Floyer family. Dr John Floyer is best known for his early studies of the human blood circulatory system. The house was pulled down in the mid-1960s. This picture dates from around 1910.

Sir Francis Lawley built Canwell Hall, seen here in 1910, on the site of a former priory. It was the Lawley family home for many years but after the First World War it was purchased by the City of Birmingham and used as a convalescent home for soldiers.

Canwell Hall from the air, showing its extensive grounds. At the time this picture was taken, around 1921, the hall was in use as a babies hospital.

Middleton Hall was once the home of the Willoughby family, which over the years had a number of distinguished members. The first was the explorer Sir Hugh Willoughby. He has the distinction of being the first Englishman to tread Russian territory reached from the sea on August 23 1553. The hall is pictured here as it was approached from the driveway, *c.* 1907.

Middleton Hall as seen from the gardens at the rear in 1905. The hall's other resident of note was Francis Willoughby. He was an accomplished naturalist and made significant contributions to the science of natural history, as we know it today. The hall is now open to the public at various times throughout the year.

The once splendid Elford Hall would have had a great many staff working there and it is one of these staff who sent this card to a friend in 1908. She was a girl called Elsie and she states to her friend that she has been out picking bluebells that afternoon and she would try to send a view of the hall showing the window of her room next time.

Well, Elsie was true to her word and here on this postcard to the same friend in 1909 she has marked her window on the top floor above the main doorway with a cross. Unfortunately the hall is no longer standing. It fell into disrepair after its owner gave it to the Corporation of Birmingham when he himself could no longer manage the financial upkeep of the house. It was demolished in 1964.

In 1872 Thorpe Hall was the residence of the Revd George Inge MA. He owned nearly all the land in the village and was Lord of the Manor. The picture shows the hall in around 1902.

Thorpe Hall, pictured in 1904, was originally built around 1680. As with most great houses later additions were built during the life of the house. A North Wing was added around 1800 and the South Wing was added in 1812. A billiard room was a further enhancement made in 1880.

Moat House, Tamworth

Bygone scenes of tranquillity as two gardeners tend to the grounds of the Moat House in Lichfield Street in 1905. During its long existence the Moat House has played host to royalty: in 1619 Prince Charles stayed there while he and his father King James visited Tamworth. King James stayed at the castle as the guest of Sir John Ferrers.

40623. Tamworth, Moat House.

The blinds are all down here on what must have been a glorious summer day in 1913 when this picture was taken of the rear of the Moat House. The net of a tennis court is just visible at the bottom of the picture. The house has not always been a private dwelling, it was used as a lunatic asylum for a number of years. The Comberford family constructed the present Moat House during the 1570s, although there was a house on the same site prior to this.

Hall End Hall during more prosperous times, probably in 1910. A large number of seats can be seen set out in front of the tennis court in this picture probably ready for a local event of some description such as the Pit Revels which were held at the hall.

Hall End Hall

George Corbyn originally built Hall End Hall, seen here in 1905. He was the squire of Hall End from 1584 until 1636. During the eighteenth century the hall was occupied by one of the joint owners of Hall End colliery, Mr C.A. Morris. In 1947 the hall came into the possession of the National Coal Board and from then on it was left unoccupied and fell into disrepair. The rotting shell of this once fine house was finally pulled down in 1969.

Hall End Farm, pictured here in 1909, was formerly known as Holt Hall.

Weeford is four miles west of Tamworth. The Revd Robert Cowpland, who was the rector for Weeford and Hints, lived here in 1872. This picture shows the rectory in Weeford, c. 1907.

This large imposing house once belonged to Tamworth's town clerk and was situated quite near to the fountain in Upper Gungate. It was demolished some time during the 1960s.

Amington Hall in 1908. The hall was once the home of a local JP, Mr C.B. Leigh Esq. He was living here in 1874. It has also been home to the Repington family.

Shenstone Court viewed from its gardens, c. 1911.

This imposing property was once the residence of Mr R.P. Cooper Esq. It is seen here in 1911.

Grendon Hall was once the home of Sir George Chetwynd. After he acquired the hall, which was then in a state of neglect, he made numerous improvements and added greatly to its size. This picture dates from 1910.

Sir George was an avid collector and the hall housed a fine library and extensive collections of coins and art. The Grendon Hall estate came up for sale in July 1931 but the hall itself was withdrawn from the sale at the last moment.

Eight
The Castle and Grounds

The seemingly ever changing castle grounds. The tennis courts depicted here in the 1930s have now given way to the bowling green, which is typically teeming with bowlers on a warm summer's afternoon.

TAMWORTH CASTLE UNDER FLOODLIGHT

The castle after it was first floodlit in 1931. It must have stood out very eerily in those days when there was not as much street and road lighting as there is today to detract from the effect.

TAMWORTH CASTLE ENTRANCE.

The ivy-clad castle lodge, shown here in 1910, was originally built by the second Marquis Townshend in 1810. On the left of the picture are seen the anchor and cannon balls which are also included elsewhere in the book in a picture of the Clock Tower at Drayton Manor.

The castle's mill is clearly visible on the right of this picture from 1915. The mill was once in the possession of the Peel family. Tamworth Rural District Council gradually acquired the mill and its surrounding buildings over a period of time in order to put in place flood prevention measures. In 1909 some of the mill's outbuildings were demolished, followed some years later by the demolition of the mill itself in 1920.

The Herringbone Masonry wall at Tamworth is said to be one of the finest examples of such masonry in the country. It probably dates from Norman times and is between ten and twelve feet thick.

The main doorway into Tamworth castle, seen here in 1909, has the coat of arms of the Ferrers family carved in stone above it. This family occupied the castle for hundreds of years and various members of the family are buried in St Editha's church. These include Sir Thomas Ferrers, who was knighted in 1461, and Sir John Ferrers who was High Steward of Tamworth.

A heavily laden cart trundles along a peacefu Holloway while a man with his bicycle stops to strike a pose in this early view, c. 1909.

A magnificently carved fireplace in the oak room at Tamworth castle, pictured here in 1910. It was carved from Irish Bog Oak with the arms of the Ferrers family. It was installed in the castle sometime in the early 1800s but it is possible the piece was carved much earlier than this.

Oak Room, Tamworth Castle

BANQUETING HALL, TAMWORTH CASTLE.

The banqueting hall in Tamworth castle pictured in 1910. This magnificent room was at one time used as a blacksmith's forge.

The castle and lodge shown after a fairly substantial snowfall in 1915. Although winter scenes like this can look attractive the cold weather can also bring tragedy. Two of the author's young ancestors were drowned in 1894 while sliding on the frozen river just yards from where this photograph was taken.

An evocative winter scene showing the castle lodge and Lady Bridge in the background, c. 1904.

An early view of the castle grounds including the bandstand that was constructed in 1900. This card was sent as a birthday card in 1904.

'The Castle', says the caption on this 1908 card, although in this instance the castle is obscured by trees and barely visible. The picture does however show some of the castle mill, on the right-hand side of the photograph.

Castle Pleasure Grounds, Tamworth.

The castle grounds in this picture seem to go on forever as they disappear into the distance. This picture must have been taken after 1937, probably during the 1940s, as the outdoor swimming baths are clearly visible.

TAMWORTH CASTLE PLEASURE GROUNDS

The large chimney just visible on the left-hand side of this picture, taken in 1950, was 300 feet high. It belonged to Fisher's Paper Mill at Kettlebrook. This site later became Turners asbestos cement (TAC) factory.

84

The new bridge across the river in the castle grounds. This bridge replaced an earlier wooden structure in 1930.

One of Hamel's Tape Mills, which was situated to the rear of George Street, can be seen at the far end of this picture taken in the castle grounds during the 1940s.

An appreciation of the commanding position of the castle can be gained from the viewpoint from which this picture has been taken, c. 1912.

The courtyard of the castle with its ancient ivy clad brickwork is captured here on a postcard produced by one of the town's printers and publishers, c. 1910.

Nine

Around the Town

One of a series of watercolours of the town, painted by artist W.G. Holt. This view shows the approach to the town from Bolebridge and dates from around 1906.

This picture was taken from near Bolebridge in 1908. Looking carefully on the left it is just possible to make out the bandstand in the castle grounds. Hamel's Mills at the rear of George Street are also visible. One of the young boys in the foreground has his shoes and socks removed as if to paddle in the river. Further along the bank young children can be seen wading across a shallower part of the river.

The railway viaduct clearly visible in the background of this picture from the 1920s was built in 1839 and is known locally as The Nineteen Arches. It was the father of the railway system himself, George Stephenson, who drove the first train across this new viaduct. Much of the stone used in this vast construction came from local quarries. In this picture there are two contrasting modes of transport: while a modern steam train speeds over the viaduct above a horse and cart emerge from the arch below.

Bolebridge from a high vantage point in 1911. The bridge in the picture was replaced by a new one in 1935. The river shown here is quite low, however Bolebridge Street was notorious for flooding before the town had proper flood prevention schemes in place. The house visible across the bridge with the gable-end wall painted white carries an advertisement for William Jenson who was a local wine and spirit merchant based at No. 5 George Street.

Dominating this 1905 view of Church Street is the large grocery shop that was run by Alfred Sadler and occupied this spot for over thirty years. As his business grew he eventually occupied No. 1, 2 and 3 Church Street.

The Paregoric shop in all its glory. The large entrance on the left of the shop doorway led off to Marshall's Yard. In 1934, fourteen years after this picture was taken, the town lost one of its finest architectural assets when the Paregoric shop was pulled down.

The Church Street side of the old Middle Entry is shown here in 1910. It ran through to Market Street at the other end. This was another one of the town's half-timbered gems that is now lost.

A view from 1905 of Church Street showing the fine half-timbered building that was the Paregoric shop. Just a little further down is the public baths and institute that was one of the many gifts to the town from the Revd William Macgregor. These were built at Macgregor's own expense in 1885 and designed to blend in with the existing architecture in the street.

Church Street, Tamworth as it was during the 1930s, before the lamentable destruction of many of its finest buildings. The Paregoric shop took its unusual name from an item sold on the premises. A Paregoric Elixir is described in the *Oxford English Dictionary* as, 'a camphorated tincture of opium flavoured with aniseed and benzoic acid'. This was often taken to relieve pain and sooth coughs. The church is seen here behind its high walls and iron railings which have since been removed.

Free Library, Tamworth

Tamworth's Free Library, seen here in 1914, was built with money provided by the great American philanthropist Mr Andrew Carnegie. He provided £2,000 for this building in 1905. Prior to this there had been other libraries in the town but these charged for membership and many people simply could not afford the fees.

This view remains very much the same today. The fact that the Territorial Army drill hall can be seen on the left of the picture dates this photograph to some time after 1911, the year this hall was built.

George Street, in around 1904 with carts three abreast in the road. On the left of the picture can be seen the butcher from Eastman's shop posing for the camera in his starched white apron.

Two young ladies can be seen strolling along George Street inthe fashions of the day, *c.* 1905.

Horses and carts go busily about their business in George Street. On the right of the picture is Thornburns boot and shoe market and next door to this, continuing down the street, is Pearkes Provision Stores. On the opposite side of the road is Eastman's the butchers and nextdoor is The New Empire pub. This pub was probably in the hands of Rosanna Bircher at the time this picture was taken in 1913.

Joseph Frisby's boot and shoe shop is visible here on the left-hand side of the street in 1906. Note the two men in this shot by the horse and cart, one with brush the other with shovel, presumably cleaning up after their transport! If only it were as easy today.

On the left of this picture from the 1940s can be seen Oliver's Hotel, a well-known establishment that was run by Oliver Boonham for well over twenty years. Opposite is Lloyds Bank and Burtons shop, both of which have remained relatively unchanged over the years.

The building on the right in this 1930s picture, Timothy Whites and Taylors the Chemists, shows off some of the work produced by a local company called Gibbs and Canning who were based in Glascote. They produced a wide range of decorative items as well as more mundane wares such as drainpipes. Just visible further along on the same side of the street is another of the company's contributions to local architecture, namely the statue that topped off the Grand Theatre. This statue was saved when the building was demolished and is now housed in the castle museum. Note also how precarious the window cleaner looks with his ladder perched on the edge of the pavement as he hangs on to the bay of the upper window.

The cottage hospital, pictured in 1905, came into being thanks to the generosity of one of the town's great benefactors William Macgregor. In 1880 he gave over £1,000 to build the hospital, which at first had only six beds available for the sick. The hospital was enlarged and improved on a number of occasions in the years that followed.

A rare glimpse of the Tamworth Co-operative Store in Lichfield Street some time during the 1920s or 30s. Notice the sign in the window declaring a dividend of 1/4 in the pound. Although the sign above the main entrance says tailoring the shop windows appear to be full of fruit and vegetables. This shop is still in existence today although it is no longer run by the Co-op. The man who founded the town's Co-operative Society in 1886 was William MacGregor. At the time this made him extremely unpopular with the local shopkeepers because of the dividend discount system it operated.

HUTTON FOUNTAIN, TAMWORTH.   165 S.BART

The fountain, pictured here in 1905, was given to the townsfolk of Tamworth by Mrs Hutton in 1898 as a memorial to her husband. It had troughs for animals to use and cups for the use of the thirsty traveller. It is also said that tramps made use of the facility to wash in before proceeding a little further down the road for a bed for the night at the town's workhouse.

The fountain must have been a welcome sight to many travellers with its softly glowing lantern on top breaking up the darkness. Behind the gentleman on the right of the picture behind the trees, stands the Queen Elizabeth's Grammar School. This picutre was taken around 1910.

LADY-BANK TAMWORTH.

A view from the 1950s still readily recognisable today. On the right is the Castle Hotel and Garage and on the left is the building that once housed the Tamworth Savings Bank. The building at the end of the road with the Bass sign on the wall was for many years the Peel Arms. This has now been incorporated into the modern hardware store that occupies the building.

VICTORIA ROAD, TAMWORTH.   167. S. BARTLE

The pub on the right of this picture from 1910 is the Tweedale Arms. This was named after the wife of the third Sir Robert Peel, who married the daughter of Lord Tweedale. Like Sir Robert his wife had a passionate interest in horse racing and gambling and it was this that ultimately led to Sir Robert's downfall.

A postcard published by local newsagent Charles Young. In all probability it is he and his family standing outside the newsagents shop in this picture, *c*. 1905.

A group of children play outside the gates of the Wesleyan chapel in Victoria Road during 1904. Victoria Road, along with Albert Road, was named in honour of Queen Victoria and Prince Albert's visit in 1843. Sir Robert Peel entertained the royal couple at his Drayton Manor home.

The railway station at Tamworth served the town's two railway lines, the upper and the lower level. The Birmingham and Derby Junction Railway were the first to arrive in 1839. Their line was the lower level line. This was followed by the upper level line of the Trent Valley railway built in 1847. This station was demolished in the 1960s.

Ten
Hopwas and Hints

A scene still readily recognisable today at Hopwas although the road looks rather bare with the distinct absence of white lines everywhere. A barely discernable sign on the wall of the house on the right refers to Hopwas Sand Pits which were just a little further along the road past the Red Lion Inn. Part of the inn is just visible in the background in this picture from the 1930s.

HPW.8   THE CHEQUERS AND CROSS ROADS, HOPWAS

Looking towards Hopwas from Tamworth during the 1950s, the Chequers (now The Tame Otter) pub is on the left of the picture. The road to the right of the zebra crossing is School Lane. which leads to a further canal bridge and the canal towpath to Hopwas Woods.

PUMPING STATION,
HOPWAS, TAMWORTH.
COPYRIGHT.

Hopwas Pumping Station came into existence because of legislation for clean drinking water to be provided for all. The first borehole was sunk in 1879 and this yielded a million gallons of water a day. A second well 189 feet deep was sunk in 1933 to provide yet more water for the ever growing needs of industry and the people of Tamworth. This postcard dates from around 1906

Looking towards Hopwas from the Tamworth side of the bridge, *c.* 1930.

School Lane in Hopwas, with its jumble of small cottages, seen here during the 1930s.

A scene of rural tranquility in Hopwas, pictured in the 1930s.

This sturdy stone bridge, which spans the river Tame at Hopwas was constructed in the early 1800s. This postcard view is from the 1930s

Hopwas village post office sometime in the 1930s.

Lichfield Road in Hopwas, shown in this picture from the 1930s. The church of St Chad's can be seen in the background, on the right.

These cottages on the roadside at Hints are still in existence today, eighty years after this photograph was taken. One of the author's relatives was given the chance of purchasing one of them, many years ago, for the princely sum of £80.

Hints Ford across Bourne Brook in 1910. Evidence of Roman occupation has been found around this area. Coins and signs of early metal working have both been discovered.

Eleven
Other Local Village Scenes

Tollhouses like this one at Atherstone in 1905 were once a familiar site on roads all around the country. There was also one situated near Lady Bridge in Tamworth and another on the Kettlebrook Road. Monies raised from these tolls were used for the upkeep and improvements of the adjacent roads.

A tranquil scene captured at the turn of the century. Along the canal, a mile or so to the left of where the man is sitting, is Fazeley Junction. It was here that William Tolson chose to build his great mill, right next to this watery highway.

Hill-Side and Hill-Top, Clifton Campville.

The village of Clifton is mentioned in the Domesday Book. At this time it was a very prosperous area, with two mills, owned by the King himself. The village acquired the second part of its name from a family of Norman descent during the thirteenth century. Note the mother and young boy posing proudly for their picture to be taken by the gate of their cottage, some time during the 1920s.

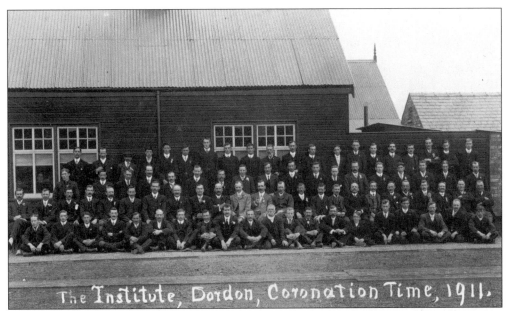

The tin-roofed hut that was the Dordon Institute in 1911. The caption reads Coronation Time so this gives a precise date for the picture of 23 June 1911 when George V was crowned at Westminster Abbey. Thousands throughout the country celebrated this event.

A group of likely lads on the Coppice Corner at Dordon, c. 1924.

A tranquil view of bygone Dosthill in 1918, long before the housing developments of recent years were built.

Dosthill High Street in 1944 looked distinctly quieter than it does today.

The absence of traffic in Dosthill is again remarkable in this photograph from the 1940s.

Main Sreet, Dosthill probably in the 1940s and at a time when the horse and cart was still as common as the motor car .

Edingale, pictured in 1915, is a small village approximately six miles north east of Tamworth. Probably the best known resident of the village was the late Mr Jos Holland. He lived in the village for over seventy years and was renowned for the shire horses that he bred here.

It would seem that most of the inhabitants in this row of cottages turned out to pose for the photographer when he took this picture, c. 1915.

Atherstone Street in Fazeley, looking towards Two Gates, in 1913. The shop on the right belonged to John Hollingshead, a boot and shoemaker. In the middle distance on the left-hand side of the road can be seen a sign for the White Horse pub, kept by William Thomas Beard.

A group of Boy Scouts from Fazeley pose proudly outside their tents in 1915. This trip was probably a great treat for them all especially as the First World War was going on and their families would have had little money to spare for such outings. The Fazeley Boy Scouts also took part in the public procession during the 1913 Millenary celebrations, along with other troops from Tamworth and Glascote.

Quite a crowd gathered to pose for this picture. It is a sign of the times that they were all able to stand across the middle of the main road through Glascote unhindered by traffic, c. 1913.

This picturesque country rectory with its tennis court in the garden, pictured in 1920, was once the home of John Bellingham Swann. He lived here during the 1880s.

This fine building was built by the Bass Brewery Company in 1932 and photographed soon after. The sign just visible on the tree on the right declares The Mile Oak Hotel open all day selling, 'Luncheons Hot and Cold, 12 til 2-30'.

A patrolman waits patiently here for some traffic to direct at Mile Oak crossroads. He certainly would not have long to wait today as the volume of traffic has increased many times since this picture was taken in the 1920s.

HOTEL AND CROSS ROADS, MILE OAK.

This picture from the 1930s shows off quite well the distinctive shape of the newly opened Mile Oak Hotel.

Home delivery the way it used to be, with a team of magnificent shire horses at Newton Aggis, c. 1905.

Newton Regis at the turn of the century is everyone's idea of a typical village with a half-timbered thatched cottage and the ancient church of St Mary's standing in the background.

A view from the 1920s, of Kettlebrook Road near Tamworth. The shop in the picture is mentioned in early copies of Kelly's Directories and was there from at least 1912 to 1936. The owner is stated to be Albert Morrall a hairdresser by trade. The houses are still in existence today. The shop today is Kettlebrook post office.

Hemlingford House in Kingsbury was used as a shop when this postcard was sent in 1914. Later notes on the rear of this postcard state Osbournes shop carried out cycle repairs in the shed at the back. Further notes state that the family had four sons, George, Ivor, Jim and John.

A father and his young family seen here enjoying an outing by the river in this very pleasant location at Kingsbury. It is possbile to see that even on such an informal occasion as this a gentleman still wore his bowler hat, c. 1912.

Coventry Road in Kingsbury earlier this century, probably during the 1930s. Close inspection of this picture reveals that the shop on the left-hand side of the half-timbered building was an agent for Midland Red Parcels, while the grocers in the foreground sold Golden Meadow Butter and Cadbury's Chocolate.

There has been a mill of some description at Kingsbury from at least the time of the Doomsday Book. During the nineteenth century it was used to produce gun barrels. Since then it has also been used at various times as a saw mill, leather mill and paper mill. This picture dates from the 1960s.

Pooley Hall stands in its imposing position alongside the river Anker at Polesworth in 1912. The hall was rebuilt in the sixteenth century by Sir Thomas Cokayne

The picturesque Polesworth Square with the Chetwynd Arms Hotel in the background during the 1930s.

This cottage was to become known nationwide through a poem written about one of its young occupants by Edward 'Ned' Farmer. He wrote a poem called 'The Colliers Child' that was used by Victorian children learning to read. There is a memorial to Farmer in the churchyard of St Editha's in Tamworth. The cottage was known as Litltle Jim's Cottage.

An almost 'Chocolate Box' scene with half-timbered buildings and thatched cottages in Bridge Street, Poleworth, c. 1914.

A peaceful scene with a young couple rowing on the river Anker. In all likelihood the boat that they are in was probably hired from the boathouse in the castle grounds, *c.* 1918.

Mr A.H Smith left no-one in any doubt that he was the landlord at the Two Gates Inn during the 1930s. This fact is declared in large letters upon the wall of the pub on the left of the picture. In one of the rear gardens of the houses on the same side is what appears to be a quite substantial pigeon loft.

Polesworth post office is on the left in this 1920s picture. On the opposite side of the road is a local shop covered in the old advertising signs so prized by collectors today. Parked outside the post office is a motorcycle and sidecar with the number plate OA 34 34.

A small section of the Roman Watling Street shown here in the 1940s with Wilnecote parish hall on the left-hand side. This building was opened in January 1932.

A young lad strikes a pose on Quarry Hill, Wilnecote at the turn of the century. Some of the stone quarried here during the nineteenth century was used in repair work carried out on St Editha's parish church in Tamworth.

Quarry Hill in Wilnecote. This view is looking along Watling Street towards Dordon. The Queen's Head pub is on the left of the picture, c. 1908.

Watling Street shown as it runs part of its long straight course through Wilnecote. The photograph is from either the 1930s or 40s.

FOR GOD,
OUR KING
AND
COUNTRY

SOLDIERS' HOME

This building was once the grandstand to Whittington Racecourse until the Army made use of it as a soldiers home. In its heyday the racecourse was very popular, two notable visitors being King Edward VII and Sir Robert Peel. The building continued in use as a barracks until 1955 when it was taken over as the clubhouse of Whittington Golf Club. The patriotic slogan printed on this postcard probably gives it a date of around 1914.

DEPÔT, ORDERLY ROOMS & ARMOURY, LICHFIELD BARRACKS.

A soldier stationed at Whittington Barracks during the First World War posted this card. The postmark states ,Whittington Barracks 9th Oct 1916. A number of soldiers can be seen on the balcony on the right of the picture.

MILITARY HOSPITAL, LICHFIELD BARRACKS.

Young soldiers pose outside the gates of the Military Hospital at Whittington in 1914. Vast numbers of soldiers were injured during the 1914-18 War and over 900,000 British and Empire soldiers lost their lives during the same period.

A rare photograph taken inside the barracks recreation room showing the men were well catered for with snooker tables and a makeshift table tennis table. From the appearance of the light fittings it would seem the place had gas lighting when this photograph was taken in 1910.

The hospital shown here at Whittington Barracks in 1914 was a very busy place during the First World War, when it treated many soldiers injured in the conflict.

The church parade in 1918 at Whittington Barracks, with troops from the Cheshire Regiment taking part. The small boys marching alongside seem to be thoroughly enjoying themselves.

An artist's impression from the 1960s of the old Wigginton Hotel. It has now been replaced by a modern public house.